T0278142

PAST & PRESENT

RICHMOND

OPPOSITE: Once located at the intersection of San Pablo and Macdonald Avenues was the Richmond archway sign that illuminated the way to Downtown Richmond and Richmond's Auto Ferry Terminals. With the city's growth and progression after the World War II effort, the addition of the Richmond-San Rafael Bridge in the 1950s ultimately led to the sign's dismantlement, shown in the image at right. (Courtesy of Richmond Museum of History & Culture.)

PAST & PRESENT

RICHMOND

Desiree Heveroh and Victoria Stuhr

Dedicated to our "City of Pride and Purpose," Richmond, California, along with its pioneers and buildings that we got to know along this journey. Your memories live on in this book and in our hearts.

Copyright © 2024 by Desiree Heveroh and Victoria Stuhr
ISBN 9781-4671-6193-0

Library of Congress Control Number: 2024941850

Published by Arcadia Publishing
Charleston, South Carolina

Printed in the United States of America

For all general information, please contact Arcadia Publishing:
Telephone 843-853-2070
Fax 843-853-0044
E-mail sales@arcadiapublishing.com

Visit us on the Internet at www.arcadiapublishing.com

ON THE FRONT COVER: East Brother Light Station was built in 1873, predating the 1905 incorporation of Richmond by 32 years. It is the oldest wood-frame lighthouse operating in the United States. It is listed in the National Register of Historic Places and is a California Registered Historic Landmark. Since 1980, it has served as a bed-and-breakfast getaway. It is particularly special to author Desiree Heveroh, who served as a light station keeper for 14 months during the COVID-19 pandemic. (Past, courtesy of Richmond Museum of History & Culture; present, courtesy of Christian Wimmer.)

ON THE BACK COVER: This 36-foot-high and 100-foot-long sign was built on a discarded barge by the Spiersch Brothers in February 1911. It was towed up the Sacramento and San Joaquin Rivers to advertise Richmond and would stay at each town for a day before moving on. (Courtesy of the Point Richmond History Association.)

CONTENTS

ACKNOWLEDGMENTS

I will try to keep my boundless gratitude as short as a perpetually verbose person can! I would like to thank my hometown of Richmond, California, for seeing the potential in me and trusting me as the keeper of so many of its historical treasures—East Brother Light Station (the great love of my life), SS *Red Oak Victory* (we went viral together), the Hotel Mac (my home in "the Point"), the Richmond Museum of History & Culture (who we nursed back to health), the Rosies (without your pioneering gumption, I might not be where I am today), and Henry J. Kaiser (whose indelible influence made Richmond full of history for those of us who care). I thank the Universe for bringing an unassuming but wildly capable magician named Victoria into my world! I hope we always make magic together.

—Desiree Heveroh

As a third-generation Richmonder, I wish to thank my family, especially my history-loving parents, for instilling in me the deep love that I have for this city. I am forever grateful to my *tío* Scott for entrusting me with my *tía* Lola's researching tools. Thank you, Richmond Museum of History & Culture, for being my home away from home, and thank you to Desiree for inviting me along on this magical and eye-opening adventure and for the constant support over these past few years.

—Victoria Stuhr

A mutual message of thanks to some special people and places that helped us along the way: Richmond Museum of History & Culture (RMHC), Point Richmond History Association (PRHA), Richmond Public Library (RPL), Capt. Jarrod Ward, Christian Wimmer, and the powers that be at Winehaven & Richmond Fire Training Academy who granted us access to take photographs. Shout out to the staff at Biancoverde at the Hotel Mac and Casper's Hot Dogs for keeping us fed whilst we toiled away.

—Desiree Heveroh and Victoria Stuhr

All past images are credited in the captions. All present-day photographs were taken by the authors unless otherwise stated.

INTRODUCTION

Richmond, California, is a unique city that is centrally located to San Francisco, Oakland, Berkeley, Napa, Marin, San Rafael, and the Greater Bay Area. It has 32 miles of Shoreline and some of the most pleasant weather all year round. A wide range of transportation options are available to its residents, including the ferry, Bay Area Rapid Transit (BART), Alameda-Contra Costa Transit District (AC Transit), Amtrak train, and Richmond Moves.

Though the original inhabitants of this area predate photography, there are artifacts that have been found marking the time of the Ohlone people. They showed great respect to the land, ensuring their creations (structures, clothing, vessels, etc.) could return to the earth leaving it virtually unaltered. An exception to this being the Shellmounds, which significantly changed the landscape of the area. The Ohlone were eventually pushed northward during the California Gold Rush, with early pioneers excavating and leveling the mounds and thus removing what little traces of the Ohlone were left to make room for a new era of industry. Richmond was a town forged with a very industrious spirit. From 1901 to 1913, the population grew from 100 to 20,000. It was touted as "the City with a Future" and "Richmond: Where Ocean Fleets and Great Railroads Meet" in all the business advertisements. Prominent community members made marks that one can still catch glimpses of today—if you know what to look for.

During World War II, there was another boom to the population, which quadrupled in three years, helping to make it one of the original melting pots of the nation. Folks came from far and wide to get a good-paying job in the shipyards, the Ford Plant, Standard Oil (later Chevron), and the Santa Fe Railroad. A wonderful ripple effect happened when Henry J. Kaiser started building ships in Richmond, the result of which was a mix of people, food, culture, religion, music, and traditions. He provided medical care to shipyard workers, resulting in the Kaiser Permanente known today. Women in the workplace developed a "We Can Do It" spirit that resulted in generations of girls who do not have to place limits on their aspirations.

Currently, Richmond hosts the only Rosie the Riveter Museum in the United States, a historic district with over 300 buildings, a functioning lighthouse from the 1800s, the oldest park ranger in the National Park Service (Betty Reid-Soskin), and the last remaining World War II Victory ship built here in our shipyards (SS *Red Oak Victory*). Richmond still holds the record for the fastest ship built—the SS *Robert E. Peary* in 4 days, 15 hours, and 29 minutes.

We are honored to be able to craft this new edition of the Past & Present series with a love that only two Richmond-native daughters dedicated to preserving history could. We got to know our city on a much deeper level. Ghosts of pioneers past have become very real to us. There were so many buildings and so many people that we wanted to include in this book. Relevant material and accurate information were not always readily available or easy to locate. We want to encourage readers who have these kinds of items to make them accessible to your local resource locations. They deserve to get their names and their stories back.

POINT RICHMOND, NATIONALLY REGISTERED HISTORIC DISTRICT

As one of Richmond's pioneer industries, Standard Oil Company, originally the Pacific Coast Oil Company, established its refinery in 1901. Originally known as East Yard, Point Richmond became a burgeoning community of refinery, port, and railway workers. Officially incorporated in 1905, it is now a nationally registered historic district, and the refinery, now called Chevron, is a polarizing fixture amongst its citizens. (Courtesy of RMHC.)

Construction of East Brother Light Station began in 1873 to provide aid to maritime navigation between San Pablo and San Francisco Bay and still does so today. Owned by the Coast Guard, the station's costly maintenance resulted in the threat of it being demolished and replaced by an automated pole. A nonprofit was founded in 1978 to save and restore the station. Since 1980, it has delighted guests as a one-of-a-kind destination getaway bed-and-breakfast. (Past, courtesy of PRHA; present, courtesy Capt. Jarrod Ward.)

Originally built in 1900, the first hotel in the area was owned and operated by the Critchett family on Washington Avenue. The land was provided by John H. Nicholl, who requested a proper establishment be available for employees of the Santa Fe Railroad. The hotel also served as the first city hall where the first board of trustees meeting was held on August 14, 1905. It is currently the Point Richmond Market. (Courtesy of PRHA.)

In partnership with his brother-in-law and fellow pharmacist Charles Edward Niedecker, Augustus Charles Lang founded the Lang Drug Company on Washington Avenue in 1901. As their company expanded, they were noted to have the biggest stock in Contra Costa County and offered a free delivery system. They would ultimately provide the foundation for Richmond's pharmaceutical businesses for many decades. The building is currently privately owned. (Courtesy of RMHC.)

A total of 20 cottages once bordered the train tracks on what was originally called First Street, now known as Oregon Street, and were originally home to the workers of the Santa Fe Railroad. The double line of houses, built in 1901, gained the nickname "Smokey Row" as a result of smoke emitted from the chimneys of passing trains landing on the rooftops. A handful of these buildings remain throughout town as homes, though relocated and renovated. (Courtesy of PRHA.)

The Bank of Richmond opened its doors in 1902, serving as the city's first bank. Beside it is the Nicholl Building, constructed by the John Nicholl Company in 1908, which was the second city hall from 1909 to 1915. The Point Masonic Lodge purchased it in 1922, staying into the 1990s. While now perennially obscured, the Nicholl Building is currently home to Summer Search Bay Area while the bank building currently houses Professional Property Management. (Courtesy of RMHC.)

Designed by architect Etienne Augustin Garin, Our Lady of Mercy Catholic Church was built for $18,000 under the supervision of the church's first pastor, Fr. Martin P. Scanlan, and was dedicated on August 23, 1903. Its Gothic Revival style included a baptistery, and the bell tower had a prominent steeple that was removed in 1934 for safety precautions. It now holds the title of the oldest church in Richmond. (Courtesy of PRHA.)

This building, constructed around 1903 and originally near Garrard Boulevard, was the employee's reading room for the Santa Fe Railroad. It was moved over slightly and became the trainmaster's building in 1944 but was ultimately left unused by 1992. Understanding that this building is possibly the last structure surviving from the original Santa Fe Depot layout, it was relocated to West Richmond Avenue and refurbished to serve as the Point Richmond branch of the Mechanics Bank in 2005. (Courtesy of RMHC.)

Built in 1904 and located at 135–137 (originally 35–37) Park Place, early occupant John Conrad Feudner and his saloon with rooming house served Point Richmond until Bert Curry converted the space into his undertaking parlors around 1909. Reverting to a tavern, Gustave Bernhard Green's Baltic Bar opened its doors in 1912. The Baltic is often reincarnated but each tenant manages to maintain its original heart and flair. It is currently known as the Baltic Kiss. (Courtesy of RMHC.)

The Peoples Water Company was founded in 1906 in Oakland and immediately became the biggest water company in the East Bay Area, gaining roughly seven constituent companies, including the Richmond Water Company. The company ultimately went bankrupt, and by 1916, it was sold to East Bay Water Company. This structure, erected in 1904, served as the Richmond branch of the water company as well as the city's pool hall and was eventually converted into an apartment building. (Courtesy of RMHC.)

Originally called First Methodist Episcopal Church, First United Methodist Church's first-ever service was held in 1900 by founder pastor William Nelson Younglove inside a Santa Fe boxcar, making it the oldest Christian church in the city. Two short-lived wooden structures were built before Rev. David Walker Calfee took charge in 1904, and with the continued help of the community, this brick Carpenter Gothic structure became the church's final iteration in 1906 and is still active today. (Courtesy of PRHA.)

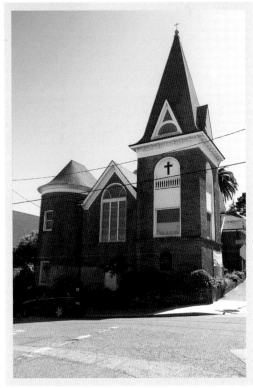

Episcopal Church on
Washington Ave.,
Built about 1908

Founded as the Trinity Episcopal Church, this two-story structure was opened for service in January 1908. The establishment of an Episcopal church in Point Richmond was pushed by the president of the Bank of Richmond and husband of land grant heiress Eugenia Emilia Tewksbury, William A. Mintzner, who donated various plots of land to the cause. It was purchased by the Dharmata Foundation in 2005. (Courtesy of PRHA.)

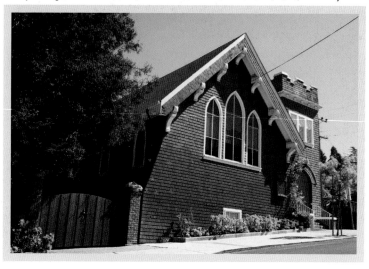

In 1908, cousins Dr. Clark Lorenzo Abbott and Dr. Ursa S. Abbott established the Abbott Hospital and Training School for Nurses on Santa Fe Avenue. The first hospital in Richmond, it was originally two stories high, but a third was quickly added in 1909 to accommodate the large volume of patients. The business was sold to the Roosevelt Hospital of Berkeley in 1913, and the structure was promptly converted into the apartment building seen today. (Courtesy of RMHC.)

The Point Richmond Triangle, encompassed by Washington Avenue, Park Place, and West Richmond Avenue, was originally considered the business center of Point Richmond. Located at the triangle's apex once stood the original "Indian" statue and fountain, which were donated in 1909 by the West Side Women's Improvement Club. After having gone missing in 1942, the statue was replicated with slight alterations and dedicated in 1984, now titled *The Sentinel*. (Courtesy of PRHA.)

This structure on Park Place was constructed in 1910 and served as Richmond's first firehouse and police headquarters. Both departments ultimately outgrew the building, with the police department leaving in 1949 for the Hall of Justice while the fire department relocated in 1961 to the current station just across the street. Privately owned since 1963, it was converted into apartments with storefronts that currently house Cherry Dog groomers and Tenax Law Group PC. (Courtesy of RMHC.)

In 1905, a once vast farm and marshland experienced rapid transformation into a small town to accommodate the multifaceted industry workers and their families. This 1910 photograph of Washington Avenue includes the People's Water Company building, Lang Drug Company, Moyles Shoes, and the Bank of Richmond. A majority of these buildings remain today thanks to citizens who care deeply about the preservation of history. Washington Avenue still serves as the main drag in Downtown Point Richmond. (Courtesy of RMHC.)

In 1911, proprietor Kate Riordan commissioned the Colonial Hotel, the first building designed by noted architect Charles Oliver Clausen and contractor James Cruickshank with plumbing provided by industry pioneers the Spiersch Brothers. It was sold to J.V. McAfee in the late 1930s and renamed the Hotel Mac. A 1971 fire left it empty until the duo Byers and Butt bought and restored it to its glory. It currently serves as a quality hostelry and fine-dining establishment. (Courtesy of the PRHA.)

Owned by Richard Tscherassy, the Point Theater was also designed by architect C.O. Clausen with James Cruickshank as contractor, making it the second building developed by the pair. It was completed on West Richmond Avenue in February 1913 and had a packed house on opening day. With the original entrance inconspicuous to the untrained eye, the side of the building is now the main entrance to the Masa restaurant. (Courtesy of PRHA.)

Also on West Richmond Avenue is the third building produced by C.O. Clausen and James Cruickshank. It was completed in August 1913 for John George Gerlach, superintendent of the Los Angeles Pressed Brick Company, whose brick product was used for its construction. The ground floor had office and bar space while the upper floors were for a hotel. After its time as the Todd Hotel, it is currently being used as an apartment building. (Courtesy of the PRHA.)

Seeing the potential Richmond had to offer, former mayor of Walnut Creek and orchard owner Eugene Blythe Anderson bought land from store owner and fellow rancher Beecher McWhorter and had this concrete building constructed in 1913. Three stories tall, the upper floors were dedicated to Anderson's Hotel and rooming house while the first floor would be used as a storefront leased to the original landowner. Today, the rooming floors are still used as apartments. (Courtesy of PRHA.)

Originally located in the Bank of Richmond Building, Beecher McWhorter's Double B Grocery Store relocated to the Anderson Building in 1913 and was advertised as a model example of modernity. The store extended the entire space of the first floor and was carefully laid out to create convenience for the customers. The storefront is currently home to Skin Esthetics and Cuts 1st Class Barbershop. (Courtesy of RPL.)

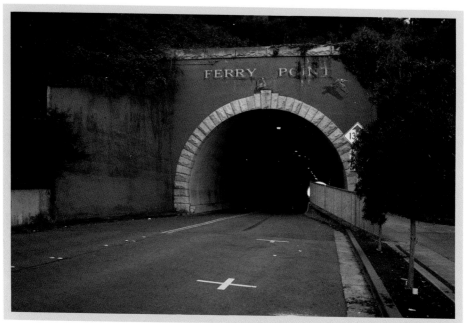

The passing of tunnel and harbor bonds allowed for the much desired addition of the Point Richmond Municipal Tunnel. It was designed by engineers Perry A. Haviland and Bert H. Tibbetts, then constructed under the Shattuck-Edinger Company. It was built in conjunction with the Municipal Wharf No. 1 and completed in October 1915. Now with murals featured on both town and shoreside entrances, it continues to be a gateway between Point Richmond and Ferry Point. (Courtesy of RMHC.)

Pictured left on the shoreside is the Santa Fe train tunnel, which was constructed under Oakland contractor Egbert B. Stone. At the time of its total completion in 1900, it originally had double tracks, making it the largest tunnel on the Pacific Coast. For 15 years, it was often used as a dangerous shortcut until the establishment of the Municipal Tunnel on the right allowed for safer access to the bay for both autos and pedestrians. (Courtesy of PRHA.)

Designed by architect James T. Narbett, Richmond's Municipal Natatorium, or "the Plunge," stemmed from John H. Nicholl, who struck an artesian well rather than oil. Nicholl donated the land around it, and the citizens of Richmond approved a bond issue to build a swim center, which opened in 1926. When earthquake damage and deterioration took their toll, Richmond citizens came to the Plunge's aid, raising the funds to have it restored before it was lost forever. (Courtesy of RMHC.)

CHAPTER

2

INDUSTRY

A competitor to San Pablo's already long-established Southern Pacific Railroad, the Santa Fe Railroad was one of the pioneer industries that put Richmond on the map right at the turn of the 20th century. The original layout of the depot, which included the railway turntable and repair shops, was dismantled and reworked over time. In 1995, Santa Fe Pacific Corporation merged with Burlington Northern Railroad, becoming Burlington Northern Santa Fe Corporation, which still operates today. (Courtesy of RMHC.)

The building located on the corner of Fourth Street and Macdonald Avenue was once home to Richmond's Polytechnic Business College, which began enrollment in 1912. Exclusive to men, this college provided business and engineering classes as well as typewriting and stenography. While the top floor housed the college, the first floor was utilized by a variety of shops, including department stores and tool shops. For many decades, it has been the Fourth Street Market. (Courtesy of RPL.)

The ambitions of brothers Edward J. and Carl Henry Burg helped shape Richmond's landscape not long after the city's incorporation. Dubbed "the Richmond pioneer real estate dealers," the Burg Brothers' Richmond office opened in August 1912 and was located on the corner of Twenty-third Street and Macdonald Avenue. They developed land tracts and sold lots to those enticed enough to purchase. Today, it houses various retail shops and apartments. (Courtesy of RPL.)

The Richmond-San Rafael Ferry Terminal operated from 1915 until August 31, 1956, the day before the Richmond-San Rafael Bridge opened. Today, all that remains are dock piles next to the bridge that rendered it obsolete. (Courtesy of RMHC.)

The Richmond-San Rafael Bridge opened to the public on September 1, 1956, linking the shores of Contra Costa and Marin Counties. It was officially renamed the John F. McCarthy Memorial Bridge in 1981, and it is still heavily used today. (Courtesy of PRHA.)

Rich-S R
Bridge
5-28-5

Completed in 1909 to open a passage from Downtown Richmond to what would eventually become the Civic Center District via Macdonald Avenue, the Southern Pacific Underpass—or "Subway," as it was called—changed transportation and led to the eventual urban sprawl and various development tracts that are still benefitting the locals in this area today. Not much has changed with the underpass, but it has been painted with murals that denote which district one is entering. (Courtesy of RPL.)

The Mechanics Bank was founded in Richmond in 1905 by Edward M. Downer, civic leader and former mayor of Pinole. This second site of the Mechanics Bank on Macdonald Avenue is a Greek Revival–style building that was constructed in 1920 and served as the bank's head office until 1980 before closing entirely by the late 1990s. The building was eventually repurposed and is the current home of the Church Iglesia De Dios Pentecostal. (Courtesy of RMHC.)

Originally known as the New Hotel Carquinez, this building was designed by architect James W. Plachek and was constructed in 1926. Renamed the Hotel Don, it originally comprised 75 rooms with first-floor storefronts and most memorably the Pinto Room cocktail lounge. It was here that city officials held negotiations with Todd-California Shipbuilding Corporation, leading to the construction of the Richmond Kaiser Shipyards. (Courtesy of RMHC.)

INDUSTRY

Part of the old downtown district off Harbour Way is the four-story, Metropolitan-style American Trust Company building. Completed in 1927 at a cost of $225,000, the basement and first floor were for bank use while the upper floors were devoted to professional offices. It is one of only two pre–World War II, multilevel buildings that remain on Harbour Way. It was later occupied by Wells Fargo Bank but is now privately owned. (Courtesy of RMHC.)

The Menghelli family's grocery store was located at Thirty-ninth Street and Macdonald Avenue and operated from the late 1920s until 1964. One of two store locations, the family rented out the second-story apartments and right-side storefront while living in a house located behind their store. The space that housed the grocery store is currently operating as a private health care facility. (Courtesy of the Menghelli family and RMHC.)

Filice & Perrelli Canning Company, founded by Genaro Filice and brother-in-law John Perrelli, moved its canning operation from Gilroy to Richmond in 1930, where it was a major employer here for 40 years. In 1959, it eventually merged with Cal-Can, made up of other large canning companies, becoming one of the largest canning cooperatives. Today, only Del Monte remains of this merger. The cannery houses various warehouses and offices. (Courtesy of RPL.)

Distinguished by a horse statue originally dubbed "Spot," Green's Boots and Shoe Repair was opened by Lewis Green on Nevin and San Pablo Avenues in 1932. The shop provided much-needed boot repairs, clothing, and horse care supplies to local horse owners and Western wear enthusiasts for over 90 years. By the early 2000s, ownership changed, and the store was renamed Golden Western Wear, a business that continues to carry on the traditions that were originally established. (Courtesy of RMHC.)

Originally constructed in 1941, this building on Cutting Boulevard was sold to Jack Newell in 1943 and was quickly expanded to house Jack Newell's Market. Newell owned various stores and taverns throughout Richmond and was known for sponsoring the city's merchant baseball teams. The building is currently home to the Richmond Food Center and, since 2011, has had a highly recognizable mural on its east wall in honor of New York's Twin Towers. (Courtesy of RMHC.)

The busy intersection shown in this c. 1950 photograph features Nelson's store located on Twenty-third Street and Macdonald Avenue. It was founded by Andrew Nelson, son of a Richmond pioneer baker, in 1940 after relocating from its original location across the street. Andrew's son Dick carried on the legacy, having a grand reopening in 1958. The store still operates to this day. (Courtesy of RMHC.)

The Richmond Greyhound Station had its origins one block away on Twenty-second Street. Operated by George Shaw, a new station on Twenty-third Street was opened in July 1942. Shaw occupied the second-story apartment and handled the daily operations of the bus station that offered travelers bus stop service, restrooms, a sparkling soda fountain, periodicals, and comfortable accommodations while waiting. Currently, La Gran Chiquita serves authentic Mexican food in this building. (Courtesy of RMHC.)

A unique business model that would have fared very well during COVID but was far too ahead of its time, Bab's Milk Depot, or simply Bab's, was a small chain of drive-in markets that sold dairy products starting in the 1960s. This particular establishment lasted a few decades before being converted into a car wash after the building had sat idle. The original sign had lasted up until recently, dimming the sense of nostalgia for many locals. (Courtesy of RMHC.)

WAR ERA

Henry John Kaiser secured government contracts for shipbuilding. Four shipyards went into full-time production, and the population of Richmond jumped from 23,000 to 100,000 in just two years, making Richmond a major player in winning the war. Kaiser shipyards produced 747 ships for the war effort, and women were employed for the first time, solidifying the iconic Rosie the Riveter image. Today, only shipyard No. 3 survived being developed over. (Courtesy of PRHA.)

Due to the planning efforts of Fred D. Parr and Richmond's first city manager, James A. McVittie, the city became home to the Ford Motor Company Assembly Plant, which was designed by industrial architect Albert Kahn in 1931. From 1942 until 1945, it shifted to wartime production, manufacturing tanks and Jeeps, as the Ford assembly line concept was the epitome of efficient production. It currently features the Craneway Pavilion, Assemble Kitchen, and Columbia Employee Store. (Courtesy of RMHC.)

Built in 1935 and capable of turning a full 360 degrees while lifting over 100,000 pounds of hefty components, the Whirley Cranes were crucial to the shipyards' task of quickly building hundreds of ships to support the war effort. After 63 years, this crane was retired and relocated to shipyard No. 3. It is currently occupied by a family of osprey (Rosie and Richie) that are monitored on live cam by the Golden Gate Audubon Society. (Courtesy of RMHC.)

Named for its neighbor, the Atchison, Topeka & Santa Fe Depot, Atchison Village was already well into construction by the Richmond Housing Authority's Defense Housing Project when the United States declared war in December 1941. Unlike other war housing built throughout Richmond, the 450 housing units within Atchison Village were constructed to last and are steadily maintained. It is managed by the Atchison Village Mutual Housing Corporation. (Courtesy of RPL.)

Completed in 1942, the first aid station provided medical care for workers in Richmond Kaiser Shipyard Nos. 3 and 4. Equipped with an X-ray machine, physiotherapy rooms, and a full-time ambulance, this prepaid medical-care concept has evolved into one of the largest health care organizations in the United States today: the Kaiser Permanente Medical Care Program, which assists current members to "Thrive." The station is now a part of the Rosie the Riveter World War II Home Front National Historic Park. (Courtesy of the Library of Congress, HAER CA-326-A--1.)

The Kaiser Field Hospital located at the corner of Marina Way and Cutting Boulevard opened in 1942 and provided health care services to Richmond's shipyard workers. It continued servicing the public from 1945 until the current Richmond Kaiser Permanente facility opened in 1995. It is a contributing property to the Rosie the Riveter World War II Home Front National Historical Park. (Courtesy of RMHC.)

This wide, single-story building, completed in 1942, served as the shipyards' sheet metal shop, riggers loft, and paint shop. Workers assigned to this location oversaw the assembly of prefabrication ship parts. Today, the building is a winery and cidery company dubbed Riggers Loft, which provides both tastings and a full view of the San Francisco Bay. (Courtesy of the Morris Wortman Collection and RMHC.)

Completed in September 1942, the machine shop was part of a series of outfitting buildings located in the Richmond Kaiser Shipyard No. 3. Propulsion machinery was assembled and polished in the machine shop, which housed the most modern tools available at that time. Remnants of the equipment remain today however, visitors can only view this historic building from the outside. The shop is now a part of the Rosie the Riveter World War II Home Front National Historic Park. (Courtesy of the Library of Congress, HAER CA-326-C-3.)

Completed in 1943, this Art Deco–style Streamline Moderne piece of architecture known as the General Warehouse was designed by Morris N. Wortman, the shipyards' chief architect, whose wartime designs were crucial to the Richmond Kaiser Shipyards. This warehouse stored common items and tools that ships were stocked with once they were completed. This building stands proudly, awaiting a new lease on life. (Courtesy of the Morris Wortman Collection and RMHC.)

Located on Florida Avenue, the Maritime Child Development Center was funded and built by the US Maritime Commission in 1943. It was one of roughly 35 locations established to help care for and educate the children of those who worked at the Richmond Kaiser Shipyards. Still integral to the community, this structure was restored in 2012 and is a part of the Rosie the Riveter World War II Home Front National Historical Park. (Courtesy of RMHC.)

Located on Cutting Boulevard, Fire Station No. 67 was commissioned by the US Maritime Commission to aid the Richmond Kaiser Shipyards. Opened in May 1943, this structure was initially meant to be a temporary structure but was transferred to the City of Richmond. Now known as Fire Station No. 7, it still services the city and is a part of the Rosie the Riveter World War II Home Front National Historic Park. (Courtesy of RMHC.)

Built in Richmond Shipyard No. 2, the SS *Red Oak Victory* was launched in 1944, serving as a fleet ammunition carrier. By 1970, she was retired in a reserve, or "mothball," fleet while all other remaining Richmond-built ships of her kind were scrapped. Returned in 1996, she has been a jewel within the Richmond Museum Association. Now berthed in shipyard No. 3, she is well cared for by volunteers while serving as a museum ship to the public. (Courtesy of RMHC.)

CHAPTER 4

COMMUNITY

Richmond's Civic Center Plaza was designed by renowned architect Timothy Ludwig Pflueger and his brother Milton Theodore Pflueger and completed in 1951. During planning, it was named Memorial Civic Center to pay homage to World War II when Richmond's population quadrupled. The plaza comprises several individual buildings that offer numerous resources for these citizens, including city hall, the Richmond Public Library, the Hall of Justice, the Memorial Auditorium, and the Richmond Art Center. (Courtesy of RPL.)

Located on Maine Avenue, the Osborne House and blacksmith shop were built by James Osborne in 1899. It took four years for him to complete the home before he could gather his family over from Sonora, California. It was sold by the family in 1969 and became an investment property. Though the blacksmith shop was torn down, the house still stands and now serves as the Veterans Resource Program. (Courtesy of RMHC.)

Located on Ohio Avenue is Wicks' Apartments, built by carpenter and manufacturer Andrew Wicks in 1902. Originally from Sweden, Wicks was one of the first pioneers of Richmond and constructed a number of homes and buildings throughout the city. The original barn structure once located beside the house temporarily served as one of Richmond's first school buildings. The house is still used as an apartment building to this day. (Courtesy of RMHC.)

This building near the corner of Fourth Street and Macdonald Avenue was once home to the undertaker company of James Garfield Clark, who moved his business to Richmond in 1912. Clark was one of the main coroners in the city and once ran for Contra Costa County's coroner position. His business in Richmond only lasted for a few years before it was relocated to Alameda. The building now serves as an apartment building. (Courtesy of RPL.)

COMMUNITY

Richmond's Carnegie Library, located at 400 Nevin Avenue, is the product of the Women's Improvement Club, which, in 1909, purchased land and applied for a Carnegie grant to establish a free public library. Completed in 1910 and twice expanded, it is one of 22 Carnegie Libraries designed by architect William Henry Weeks. This building was used as the main library until 1949. In 1963, it became the official and current home of the Richmond Museum of History & Culture. (Courtesy of RPL.)

Constructed in 1910, this building on Ohio Avenue was once home to the Allamanno family and their grocery store. A native of Italy, Alexander Allamanno operated the street-level store, which was seen as a convenience to the growing neighborhood. Though the grocery store was short-lived, the building stayed a part of the family for nearly 100 years. It is currently a multifamily home. (Courtesy of the Allamanno family and RMHC.)

Previously known as the Joseph Boyd tract, the 94-acre Grand View Terrace tract was created by the Burg Brothers around 1910. It was intended to be the finest and highest-class residential property available in Richmond. Though the fountain, featured here on Clinton Hill in 1916, no longer exists, the homes, original stone street signs, and remnants of the original street names can still be found. (Courtesy of RMHC.)

Located at Tenth Street and Bissell Avenue, St. Mark's Catholic Church was established in 1911. In May 1914, this original structure was nearly destroyed in a fire possibly caused by crossed wires. At the helm of Fr. Patrick M. Griffin, funds were raised, and the church was promptly rebuilt and reopened by August of that year. It still continues to serve the Catholic community today. (Courtesy of RMHC.)

COMMUNITY

Named for the Richmond pioneer family and original Rancho San Pablo land-grant owners, the Andrade family of Portugal, the Andrade Apartments located within the Andrade Tracts, were built on Gaynor Avenue under Herbert F. Brown in 1912. Brown was one of Richmond's prominent realty operators, getting his start by purchasing land for subdivisions. This building was heavily advertised and kept up to date with the latest features, and it still serves as apartments today. (Courtesy of RPL.)

A prominent part of the Burg Brothers tract, the Raymond Apartments located at Twenty-fifth Street and Macdonald Avenue were designed by San Francisco architect Gardner and finished in late summer 1914 to help meet the demand of the quickly growing city. While land around the structure continued to be developed, a wait-list of hopeful occupants grew. Today, it continues to serve as an apartment building with storefronts. (Courtesy of RMHC.)

COMMUNITY

Originally dubbed the Regal Apartments by the Burg Brothers, this three-story apartment building located at Twenty-third Street and Nevin Avenue was constructed in 1916. Each apartment had two or three rooms, with fully furnished options available. It was a popular choice for newly married couples. While the outer building is very much unchanged, the apartments are continuously modernized and kept up to date to this day. (Courtesy of RPL.)

Becoming their third hospital location, the Abbott cousins had the building at 912–920 Macdonald Avenue constructed in 1916 by noted Richmond contractor Mathew Morton. The building was sold in 1935 to make way for a J.C. Penney Company location on the first floor while maintaining the Abbott Emergency Hospital and offices on the second floor. It eventually became a location for Milen's Credit Jewelers and Burt's shoes by the 1950s. It is now home to Reentry Success Center. (Courtesy of RMHC.)

COMMUNITY

With the need for an additional fire company, the City of Richmond purchased two lots of land in the town of Stege (later rezoned into Richmond) from G. Griswold for $1,150. Construction started in 1916, and in 1917, Fire Company No. 4 opened with a small crew of three. Though its services were replaced by the new Bayview Firehouse, it currently provides a home for the Richmond Firefighter Training Youth Academy. (Courtesy of Christian Wimmer.)

Located on Macdonald Avenue, the Winters Building was designed by noted architect Albert Worden Cornelius for floriculturist Adolf Winters. Completed in 1923, the building housed a floral and a music shop at street level and a ballroom on the upper floor, which often hosted a variety of events and celebratory occasions. The building is still active through music and dance, serving as the home for the East Bay Center for the Performing Arts. (Courtesy of RPL.)

In 1926, the land area that included the Nicholl family ranch was acquired by the city for a public park on Macdonald Avenue. The original gate was gifted by Mary Nicholl Kruger to honor her father, John Nicholl. Though time has changed the attractions that were once available, such as an aviary and a children's train ride that are now long gone, it is still a staple location to the community. (Courtesy of the Maslov family and RMHC.)

Founded by musicians Bill Dias, Tony Scalise, and Al Dias, the Richmond School of Music opened on Twenty-third Street in 1946. The business was a combination music and dance school and musical equipment store. Bill Dias was also a radio personality on Northern California's first independent FM station, Contra Costa County's KRCC. Now located just beyond the Richmond–San Pablo border, the building is home to That Luang Market. (Courtesy of the Dias-Short Collection and RMHC.)

COMMUNITY

While Richmond's Carnegie Library was downsized to the building's basement and retitled the Fourth Street Branch, the remainder of the book collection was moved to the current Richmond Public Library located within the Civic Center Plaza. Opened in 1949, the library continues to serve the community and will begin extensive updates and renovations in 2025. The past image is from the 1967 series of the Civic Center Plaza. (Courtesy of RPL.)

This tower opened in April 1951 to provide simulated rescue training to firefighter cadets. Prior to this, practical training took place in various buildings around the city, but a 1943 fire that devastated a school left no question that a proper training facility was needed in order to be better prepared to handle fires of this magnitude. In 1950, Carl Overaa and Co. started construction on the $20,000 tower. (Courtesy of RPL.)

CHAPTER 5

FORGET ME NOTS

Once the original location of the Blume family ranchland of the 1850s, the Hilltop Mall was developed by Adolph Alfred Taubman and completed in 1976. Many believe it was the ultimate cause of the decline of Richmond's once thriving downtown. It closed in 2021, not able to withstand the closure of anchor stores and the dire impact of COVID-19. Like the rest of the buildings in this chapter, it now waits to be redeveloped or repurposed. (Courtesy of RMHC.)

Ferry Point was once the location of Santa Fe Railway's westernmost terminus. The original wooden pier was constructed in 1900 and was utilized until a fire occurred in 1984. The area then became a part of the East Bay Regional Park District in 1991. The structures, including the pier, metal gantry, pump house, and warehouse, have all sat in disrepair, but current plans to clean up and preserve what remains are in progress. (Courtesy of RMHC.)

The original Maple Hall located on Ohio Avenue was built in 1904. For just over a decade, it was used predominantly for recreational entertainment, housing a general store, saloon, dance and banquet hall, and boxing arena. It was an extremely popular destination on the weekends, especially for Richmond's socialites. By the 1920s, it had been reconfigured and the exterior simplified for apartment housing. It has now sat quietly for years. The present photograph showcases its full view. (Courtesy of RPL.)

The aftermath of San Francisco's 1906 earthquake and fire led to the relocation of the California Wine Association to Richmond. The castle-like structure, known as Winehaven, was completed in 1907 and operated until 1919 when Prohibition forced the company to sell. The US Navy took over the area from 1941 until 1995. It was successfully listed in the National Register of Historic Places and is currently used as a personal storage facility. (Courtesy of Bobby Winston.)

FORGET ME NOTS

The Calwa brand of wine produced had extensive reach thanks to the Belt Line Railroad, which was a transportation asset. It provided a direct connection between Winehaven's special electric switching service to the railroad systems of the entire state. Distant saloons could order five-gallon casks to be dropped at their local rail depots. Cargo was then carried along the wharf on an electric railway line. The once industrious tracks now sit quietly behind the majestic brick fortress. (Courtesy of RPL.)

In the early 1900s, "Cut Flower" nurseries in Richmond were operated by pioneer Japanese American families such as Oishi, Sakai, Adachi, Maida, Park, Oshima, and Ninomiya. During World War II, Executive Order 9066 forced them to uproot their thriving businesses and homes for relocation to internment camps. A few families were able to return to the area to start over. Today, these are the only surviving structures of this prolific turned poignant tale of blossoms and thorns. (Courtesy of PRHA.)

One of the many brickworks in Richmond was the Los Angeles Pressed Brick Company, which started in 1907 and supplied bricks to many local buildings and West Coast cities. It later operated as Richmond Pressed Brick Works from 1915 until 1965. Now referred to as Brickyard Cove, the area lends space to a number of houses and condos that overlook the bay. Recently, kilns and smokestacks that still stood were ordered to come down, brick by brick. (Courtesy of PRHA.)

Due to the close proximity to the Santa Fe and Southern Pacific Railroads, the Pullman Company chose Richmond as the westernmost location for its palace train car repair shops, which were completed in 1910. Experts in almost every trade were utilized to refurbish luxury train cars but ultimately, a change in society's travel habits caused the shops to close in 1959. It housed Tradeway Flooring until 2021, and the property is now privately owned. (Courtesy of RMHC.)

PULLMAN SHOPS RICHMOND, CAL.

This two-story, Classical Revival–style First National Bank building on Sixth Street and Macdonald Avenue was designed by architect W.H. Weeks and completed in 1910. It was considered a great beauty that graced Downtown Richmond. Its first floor was dedicated to the bank, while the second floor was set up for business offices. By the 1960s, it was the Central Valley National Bank, but for over a decade, the building has been unoccupied. (Courtesy of RMHC.)

Harbor Creamery was established by former Richmond mayor Otto Richard Ludewig in 1912, who sold it the following year to the Silveira brothers. In 1916, the Silveiras renamed it the Eagle Creamery Company, and it stayed in business until 1931. The Richmond Market, located on the right side, was also founded by Ludewig, who sold it in 1933. Both establishments provided the best quality dairy and meats to the city. The building currently sits idle. (Courtesy of RPL.)

Designed by architect A.W. Smith for William Mintzer, the Hacienda de San Pablo was purchased by Dr. Hendrick Nelson Belgum in 1915 with the intent of transforming it into the Grande Vista Sanitarium. Originally built in 1902, with its gardens and orchard, it was a sanctuary for those of affluent backgrounds suffering from mental illnesses. A series of fires reduced the structures down to the foundations, and the remnants can be visited on a trail in Wild Cat Canyon. (Courtesy of RMHC.)

Thomas Patrick Fahey, or "T.P. Fay" for short, was a prominent real estate broker who had made his name known up and down the West Coast. His building on Macdonald Avenue was an extended office of the T.P. Fay Company, which was headquartered in Berkeley. Alongside the Burg Brothers, he was a part of the residential boom that took place in Richmond in the early 1910s. The building is currently unoccupied. (Courtesy of RPL.)

Located near Santa Fe's old western terminal is the original Municipal Wharf No. 1. The terminal was completed around 1916, with a warehouse being added in 1919. The ferry slip provided passage to San Francisco via Southern Pacific Golden Gate Ferries, which were discontinued once the bridges to San Francisco were completed in 1936–1937. Today, the structures sit empty, and the remnants of the wharf have eroded with time and exposure to the elements. (Courtesy of RMHC.)

CALIF. ART TILE CO
RICHMOND, CAL.

The California Art Tile Company, once located at South Twenty-seventh Street and Maine Avenue, was a prominent producer of standard and decorative art tiles. They supplied tiles to businesses and private residences throughout Richmond from the 1920s into the 1950s for bathrooms, kitchens, fireplaces, or as commissioned. With their beauty still sought out, the tiles are now collectibles. The area is currently a part of Boorman Park, named for noted Richmond pioneer Benjamin Boorman Jr. (Courtesy of RMHC.)

Located on Twenty-third Street, the Richmond Hospital was founded in 1929 and expanded in 1939 when an east wing was added with modern facilities. In 1950, an additional phase of construction added the south wing to modernize it. This facility was once deemed vital to the health community but was shut down in the 1980s. The building still stands but has been boarded up and closed off to the public. (Courtesy of RMHC.)

DISCOVER THOUSANDS OF LOCAL HISTORY BOOKS FEATURING MILLIONS OF VINTAGE IMAGES

Arcadia Publishing, the leading local history publisher in the United States, is committed to making history accessible and meaningful through publishing books that celebrate and preserve the heritage of America's people and places.

Find more books like this at
www.arcadiapublishing.com

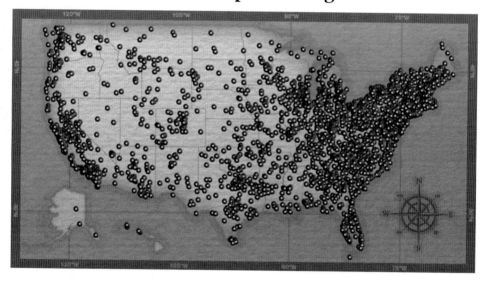

Search for your hometown history, your old stomping grounds, and even your favorite sports team.